And The Magic Truck

Susan Harris

Z and the Magic Truck

By Susan Harris

DORRANCE PUBLISHING CO., INC.
PITTSBURGH, PENNSYLVANIA 15222

This book is dedicated to Z whose love of trucks inspired this book.

His 7 cousins participated in its creation.

Special thanks to all my grandchildren, and special kudos to Mc who drew Trucky.

The contents of this work, including, but not limited to, the accuracy of events, people and places depicted; opinions expressed; permission to use previously published materials included; and any advice given or actions advocated are solely the responsibility of the author, who assumes all liability for said work and indemnifies the publisher against any claims stemming from publication of the work.

All Rights Reserved

Copyright © 2022 by Susan Harris

No part of this book may be reproduced or transmitted, downloaded, distributed, reverse engineered, or stored in or introduced into any information storage and retrieval system, in any form, or by any means, including photocopying and recording, whether electronic or mechanical, now known or hereinafter invented without permission in writing from the publisher.

Dorrance Publishing Co., Inc.

701 Smithfield Street

Pittsburgh, PA 15222

Visit our website at www.dorrancebookstore.com

ISBN: 978-1-4349-1789-8

eISBN: 978-1-4349-1708-9

Z loves trucks. He plays with trucks all during the day. At night he even dreams of trucks.

Sometimes his dad takes him on a truck ride. **really loves that.**

One day his dad even rented a Skid Steer to do some work in the yard. had the best ride ever with his dad on that.

His mom and dad would both read him books with lots of different trucks. Z knew all the names of the trucks. He wished he could ride on all of them.

One night Z was sleeping in his bed, and he heard a noise. It was a happy voice saying,

"Z, Z, would you like a ride to Truckland?"

Z wasn't sure what he was hearing. Truckland?

But then he looked up, and his room was a big truck with big eyes and a big smile. He said, "My name is Trucky, and I am a magic truck. If you hop inside my cab, I will take you to Truckland, where you will see all kinds of trucks and tractors."

Well, **Z** was a little afraid. But Trucky seemed so nice and so happy, and just imagine… going to Truckland!

So **Z** hopped in the cab. Trucky made a little toot and a puff and away they flew, out the window, above all the houses, and away. You see, magic trucks can fly.

Z was still a little afraid, but he was also very excited.

Soon Trucky landed. Oh my, what they saw. There were trucks everywhere.

Z rode in lots of trucks.

His favorite rides:

He rode in a backhoe excavator and that has a big arm to dig into the dirt. It was like a big shovel.

He rode in a fire truck and pulled the

siren. Thank goodness there was no fire.

He rode in a monster truck. He had to climb up stairs to get into it because it is sooo tall. He drove over large piles of dirt and mud and the big tires sprayed mud everywhere.

He drove a tractor just like a farmer does.

He plowed the field so corn could be planted.

And the last ride was his favorite. He loaded up the Skid Steer with fruit snacks and drove them to all of his friends to share.

What fun **Z** had riding those trucks.
Z knew this was the last ride. But hopes Trucky will come back and take him to Truckland so he can ride in more trucks.

The day was over for Trucky and and what a day it was!

Trucky Z flew back to his bed. The next morning, Z woke up and wondered if he really went to Truckland or if it was just a dream, but then he looked on his floor and there was a little truck that looked just like Trucky smiling at him.

Z knew he had really been to Truckland.

Do you think Trucky will ever come back and take **Z** again?

I guess we will all just have to wait and see.

Your child's picture can go here.

CPSIA information can be obtained
at www.ICGtesting.com
Printed in the USA
BVHW090715100722
641663BV00013B/456